RENEWING
THE
MIND
THROUGH
THE WORD

by
Bill Basansky

Harrison House
Tulsa, Oklahoma

Unless otherwise indicated all Scripture quotations are taken from the *King James Version* of the Bible.

4th Printing
Over 14,000 in Print

Renewing the Mind
Through the Word
ISBN 0-89274-023-X
Copyright © 1976 by Bill Basansky
P.O. Box 7126
Fort Myers, Florida 33911

Published by Harrison House, Inc.
P.O. Box 35035
Tulsa, Oklahoma 74153

Contents

1
Inferiority Complex

It is my desire to challenge and awaken every Christian to ask himself this question, *"Is my mind renewed in the Word of God?"*

I am not asking you whether you are Spirit filled, but I am asking you, *"Is your mind renewed in the Word?"*

Do you have any symptoms of an *unrenewed mind?*

I am going to discuss (in this booklet) several symptoms of the unrenewed mind in a Christian. As you study these symptoms and learn how to resolve them in your Christian walk, you will live a more victorious life.

Jesus has promised a victorious life to every believer who recognizes undesirable symptoms in his life, humbles himself before God and asks to be made free.

To be a mature Christian it is very important for an individual to understand and recognize symptoms of an unrenewed mind. Having recognized undesirable symptoms in your life, you must *renounce* them and not fellowship with them. (Don't give in to them.) Then renew your mind by *confessing* what the Word of God says you are in Christ Jesus. 2 Corinthians 5:17,

> **Therefore if any man be in Christ, he is a** *new creature: old things are passed away;* **behold, all things are become** *new*.

1 Corinthians 5:17

> **For he hath made him to be sin for us, who knew no sin; that** *we might be made the righteousness of God in him*.

1 Corinthians 5:21

The first symptom of an unrenewed Christian mind that we will discuss is the *inferority complex*, or a feeling of unworthiness.

5

Many Christians say, "Well, I don't *feel worthy*, and I am *afraid*."

If you are a born-again Christian, redeemed by the blood of Jesus, and being made the righteousness of God, then fear, unworthiness, and an inferiority complex should no longer be a part of your Christian life. The Word says that fear does not come from God.

> **For God hath not given us the spirit of fear; but of power, and of love, and of a sound mind.**
>
> **2 Timothy 1:7**

If you have fear to make decisions and step out for God, then, you have an *inferiority complex*, which is a symptom of an unrenewed mind.

To say, "Well, I don't think I could do that, I don't know how," or "I am embarrassed," does not mean that you are not saved or Spirit filled. It does mean that your mind needs to be renewed with the Word of God.

I can understand how you feel when you say, "I can't do it," but I cannot agree with you, for the Word says that we can do *all things* through Christ who strengthens us.

So when your mind tells you to say, "I can't," or "I'm not worthy," that is the moment you should say out loud, *"I can do all things...,"* then you will possess exactly what you *say.*

The Bible says that Jesus is loved, by the Father — equally, with you and me.

> **I in them, and thou in me, that they may be made perfect in one; and that the world may know that thou hast sent me, and has *loved them, as thou hast loved me.***
>
> **John 17:23**

God the Father loves you as much as He loves Jesus. And if God loves you as much as He loves Jesus, then the power that He gave to Jesus, He also gave to you. Jesus could raise the dead and so can you. That's right, *you!* Because the Bible says,

> **Verily, verily, I say unto you, He that believeth on me, the works that I do shall he do also; and greater**

works than these shall he do; because I go unto my Father.

John 14:12

We should not take this statement lightly, but believe the Word and then practice *doing* and *confessing* what God said we can do, for God does not lie.

"God is not a man, that He should lie...."

Numbers 23:19

2
Inability To Concentrate

Another symptom of the *unrenewed mind* is the *inability to concentrate*. Are you unable to read the Word of God without falling asleep?

Please understand, this is not a sign that you are not saved. However, it is a sign that your mind needs to be dealt with by the Word of God.

You say, "I can't stay awake."

How many times have you desired to read the Word? You plan to take a shower, or a bath, turn your night light on, go to bed and read your Bible. You had very good intentions to do that. But what happens when you get into bed?

You really mean to "study and show yourself approved unto God, a workman that needs not to be ashamed, rightly dividing the word of truth" (2 Tim. 2:15). The first thing you knew, you woke up in the night, or the next morning, and to your surprise you found your Bible on the floor. All of a sudden, when you started to read your Bible, *a sleep* that you could not control came upon you. You just had to go to sleep.

Have you had that problem? Do you know what I'm talking about?

If you do have the problem, then you need to renew your mind through the Word of God.

You see, I know these things because I have experienced them also. I am trying to tell you that when you start to read your Bible, . . .**then cometh the devil, and taketh away the word out of their hearts** (Luke 8:12).

9

The devil will use every trick that he knows to take the Word out of your heart and keep you from receiving the truth.

He *will* succeed unless *you* learn how to come against him.

You are going to have to say, "Devil, I know you. I take authority over you. I command you in the name of Jesus to depart from me."

You have to command (say) to your mind and your thoughts to "stay awake, be alert and attentive to the Word."

I know it's real! It works for me, and it will work for you, too, if you understand what to do about it. When you take authority over Satan, and *you command* him to leave in the name of Jesus, *he has to go* and your mind will be at peace.

> **Thou wilt keep him in perfect peace, whose mind is stayed on thee: because he trusteth in thee.**
>
> **Isaiah 26:3**

3

The Spirit of Condemnation

When you as a Christian — even a Spirit-filled Christian — recognize some of the symptoms of an unrenewed mind, you should not run away from them or be condemned by them. You need to come and ask Jesus to deliver you and cleanse you with His blood. The Bible says in Romans 8:1.

There is therefore now no condemnation to them which are in Christ Jesus...

If you are a child of God, don't listen to the condemnation.

Condemnation is another symptom of the unrenewed mind.

How can a Christian know if it is God talking to him, or if it is the devil condemning him?

Does God condemn? Of course not!

First of all — we read in the above scripture, ''there is now no condemnation to them which are in Christ Jesus.'' If you are a *born again believer*, then you have the wisdom of Christ Jesus in you, and you will know that it is not God condemning you. It is the other spirit that we call the devil. God does not condemn.

If you do something wrong, don't run *away* from God. Run *to* God. The Spirit of God will *gently* show you that you were wrong, and He will *lead you to repentance*. You will then know that it was wrong, and there is now no condemnation, because you repent, and God says that you are forgiven. You are washed in the blood of Jesus Christ. That's the difference. The Spirit of God does not condemn you. He points out the things wrong in your life, but He brings no condemnation with it.

11

The spirit of the devil brings condemnation, loneliness, oppression and rejection in your mind. The *way to be free* from the attack of the devil is to know *who you are* in Christ and *what authority* He has delegated to you.

You are to resist all temptations and symptoms with the Word of God, regardless of how you feel or what you see, and the devil will depart from you, just like he departed from Jesus.

However, if you allow the devil to tempt and rule you, he'll come around and put you under condemnation, because he likes to see people tormented.

Remember, the Word says in Isaiah 26:3,

Thou wilt keep him in perfect peace, whose mind is stayed on thee: because he trusteth in thee.

God said He will keep us in perfect peace, *whose mind* is upon the Lord. God trusts you and you are going to have to trust Him.

How are you going to keep your mind on the Lord?

I will use this as an example. You know how a computer works. A computer is fed with information and you have to put the proper key into the computer in order to receive the proper answer. If you put the wrong key into the computer you won't get the right answer.

Now — let's say that same computer is in your mind. What is going to happen when you wake up in the morning and look at your wife (or husband) and say, "Oh, no!" Or you look out the window and say, "Oh, no, it's going to rain again!"

When you wake up in the morning and the first thing to come out of your mouth is a negative statement or condemnation, what do you suppose is going to happen all day to you and those with whom you come into contact?

You have set the wheel of your mind in motion with *condemnation*. When you get up with a sour face, what do you think is going to happen to every person you see?

The same thing is going to happen to them. They may have a smile on their face, but when they look at you their smile drops, too, because your spirit of condemnation and heaviness is infecting them.

If a person were to come into your room and that person had a big cigar; if he *lit* that cigar and took just one puff you would smell the cigar smoke, wouldn't you? You would especially notice the smell more strongly if you do not smoke.

The same thing happens when an evil spirit is being released from a person. It is just like that smoke, it spreads throughout and attacks those who have joy.

You are going to have to realize, in a family especially, that when you get up in the morning, you must put a smile on your face, whether you feel like it or not. You smile, not because you *feel* it. *You smile because He is worthy.* When you do this, you have renewed your mind; you have *programmed* the Word into yourself, as a computer, and out comes the joy of the Lord. Condemnation or anything that is not of joy will be rejected by your computer, and now you are walking around spreading joy to other people because the Spirit of the Lord is working in you.

4
Obsessed With Prejudice

Being *"Obsessed With Prejudice"* is one of the symptoms of an unrenewed mind. You would be surprised at how many Christians are *obsessed with prejudice.*

I am not necessarily speaking of racial prejudice, although it could well be.

May I give you the definition of the word *prejudice*?

The dictionary says that *prejudice* is a "preconceived and unreasonable idea, judgment, or opinion; intolerance, suspicion, malice; skillfully trying to look for an opportunity to find things wrong about a person, and make him feel lesser than you are." That is a *prejudiced person.*

How many times have you walked into a supermarket and found yourself wanting to go around to a different aisle? You didn't want to go through a particular cash register line, because you didn't like the "checker" who was standing there.

Have you gone to a store, or perhaps a bank, and you don't like the teller or the clerk? Have you ever seen a person coming down the street, and you would turn around and walk a block out of your way, so you wouldn't have to meet him? He hasn't done anything wrong to you especially, but there's just something about him that you don't like.

If that is the case, then you need to renew your mind, because that is *prejudice* and judgment.

We are so quick to judge other people and to prounounce our judgments. Then we feel miserable! The Bible says in John 5:22,

For the Father judgeth no man, but hath committed all judgment unto the Son.

If God the Father does not judge you, what right do you have to judge another person?

If we try to take the authority away from our Lord Jesus Christ and judge other people, our judgment is not just. No wonder so many Christians are miserable.

How many times have you seen people in different denominations condemn other denominations by their words and their deeds?

They are "Obsessed With Prejudice." Their minds are not renewed. Romans 2:1 says this,

Therefore thou are inexcusable, O man, whosoever thou art that judgest: for wherein thou judgest another, thou condemnest thyself; for thou that judgest doeth the same things.

And Romans 14:4 tells us this,

Who art thou that judgest another man's servant...?

You see, we have no authority to judge anyone. The only authority that we have is to pray one for another and to love one another.

A new commandment I give unto you, That ye love one another; as I have loved you, that ye also love one another.

By this shall all men know that ye are my disciples, if ye have love one to another

John 13:34,35

What is He telling us?

He says for us to love one another, and if we love one another, then all men will know that we are disciples of Jesus.

Can you see why so many Christians are miserable?

It is because they are taking the position of a judge, and not as son or daughter. They know in their spirits that they do not have that authority, thus bringing condemnation upon themselves.

Christian friend, if you are "Obsessed With Prejudice," you need to *renew your mind with the Word.*

5
Compulsion to Perfection

Another symptom area of the *unrenewed mind* that causes many Christians to suffer is the "abnormal compulsion to perfection."

They expect an unreasonable amount of perfection in themselves, but they are never able to achieve it. The also expect perfection of everyone around them, or those who work with them, and because they do not find perfection in everyone, they are intolerable.

Some Christians have abnormal *compulsion to perfection* in their homes. I've been in some homes where you wouldn't dare to sit down on the couch unless they put some kind of quilt over it. I've been in some places where you couldn't walk on the kitchen floor unless you took your shoes off in the garage. I've been in places where they have silverware that cost a great deal of money, but the family would not use it more than once or twice a year.

These people have the *compulsion to perfection*, when they would say, "Don't touch my china. Don't sit on my couch. Don't touch my tools! Don't get into my car with those dirty hands!" This is not a complete list by any means, but each should search his own heart to see if he has such *compulsion to perfection symptoms.*

It is miserable to have a father, mother, or children who are obsessed with a compulsion to perfection. One cannot enjoy life around them, and they cannot enjoy it themselves.

God dealt with me concerning my car and my children. My children are worth more to me than the car. My house was made to live in and to enjoy, and not to die a living death, which is brought about by the compulsion to perfection.

Your house, too, ought to be a home, and not just four walls. Your floor was made to be walked upon and not to *be flown over*. The furniture that you buy is supposed to be used to sit on and to enjoy. If it gets dirty, it can be cleaned. We should enjoy what we have. Paul says,

> **Charge them that are rich in this world, that** *they* *be not highminded, nor trust in uncertain riches, but in the living God,* **who giveth us richly all things to enjoy.**
>
> **1 Timothy 6:17**

I'm not saying for you to bring dirt into the house on purpose. But, if it accidentally happens, *don't blow your cool.* In spite of all your relationship with Jesus, if you *blow your cool,* you've lost every joy, and you will cause the people around you to lose their joy. When you have a symptom of *compulsion to perfection,* and you go to pieces, the devil is right there to work on you and everyone around you.

About the worst hell on earth is to work with someone or to live with someone who has the *compulsion to perfection.* Now, I'm not saying that a person should not be neat. I'm sure you understand what I'm saying. I'm talking about those people who follow you around with a dust rag, and each time you get up they wipe off where you were sitting. You feel that you are sitting on pins and needles, and your muscles are so tense that you can't relax. The opposite is just as true, when an individual is negligent and does not pick up or clean up his own mess. This too is a symptom which is not of God.

Have you known persons like that?

Christian, if compulsion to perfection or negligence is your problem, you need to renew your mind. It is not a sign that you're not saved, but you need to renew your mind with the Word of God. You need to put priorities where they belong. God does not require that your *things* be perfect, but that *your heart* be perfect toward God and people.

6
Narrow-Mindedness

As a Christian, I am not asking if you are saved, or Spirit filled. I believe that you are washed in the blood of Christ. I am asking you to think about your mind. *Has your mind been renewed with the Word of God,* or are you suffering from *"Narrow-Mindedness?"*

Can you listen to other people's opinions? Can you stand it when other people attack your pet theories or ideas? Or, do you cut them off, give them the cold shoulder? Do you refuse to fellowship with them, to go to see them, or to talk to them?

Narrow-mindedness is a symptom of the *unrenewed* mind. You can be saved, but your mind is not yet renewed. This is why you don't know the perfect will of God. When your mind is unrenewed, God cannot direct you.

Narrow-mindedness appears in many areas. The belief in doctrines is an area where narrow-mindedness abounds. One person may say, *"Once saved, always saved,"* and another may say, *"Saved today and going to hell tomorrow."* You can get involved with doctrine instead of getting involved with Jesus.

For example, a father had two sons. One son went to one school, and the other son went to another school. One son learned, *"Once saved, always saved."* The other son learned, "Well, you're *saved today, and if you sin tomorrow, you go to hell."*

The father, who was a pastor of a particular church saw his two sons graduate. They each received a diploma from his particular school, and now they both are pastors. They came home to their father's church, and one Sunday one son taught *once saved always saved.* The next Sunday the other son taught, *saved today, and going to hell tomorrow.* The father was away for two weeks. When he returned the third week, the whole congregation was split wide open, confused, and many left the church.

Narrow-mindedness is a tool that the devil uses. Instead of you getting involved with doctrines, you ought to *get involved in loving Jesus.*

One of the most dangerous things to get involved in is the discussion of doctrines. It is not important to which denomination you belong or what doctrine that you believe in, but what is more important is, ''Who is your Father, and to which family do you belong?''

In the Old Testament, when God the Father gave a command to Moses, what did Moses do when he went to the Pharoah? What did he tell him? Did Moses say, ''Pharoah, let me come into your chambers and discuss the commandment of God?''

Instead of saying, ''Let's discuss the problem,'' Moses said, ''Let God's people go.''

God spoke to Moses. He had the *will of God in his heart,* and when he spoke to Pharoah, he said. ''Let God's people go! And if you don't, God will judge you, your people, and your nation.''

Moses did not discuss the Word. He went to proclaim the Word of God. When he proclaimed the Word of God, things began to happen, because God is behind His Word, and He hastens to perform it.

We need not discuss the Word of God. We need to go and proclaim His Word. As we proclaim the Word of God, it's up to God to do the rest.

I know that many Christians have difficulty with symptoms of narrow-mindedness, and I am not claiming to have achieved perfection. But we have to realize that when we do wrong, it is for us to humble ourselves before God and ask for His forgiveness, and then the Word will deliver us from our symptoms.

Soon after I and my wife were both saved and filled with the Holy Spirit, my wife disagreed with me about one of my decisions. I, in my own narrow-mindedness, refused to receive her thinking and became angry with her. I went to bed pouting and throwing a tantrum. I wouldn't talk to her. I didn't say "Good-night" to her. I tried to sleep, but I couldn't. I was miserable and full of anger. She was still in the kitchen taking care of the dishes, and she didn't know the attitude of my heart concerning her, for I hadn't even told her. I was lying in bed — and I huffed, and I puffed, and I even thought of leaving the house.

I'm telling you about a Spirit-filled Christian who, through his narrow-mindedness, willingly gave his mind over to the devil to be tormented.

The same thing happens to you when you give *your mind* and your thoughts over to the devil. He comes into your mind, starts tormenting you and will not let you sleep. He won't give you any peace.

This is what happened to me. I tried to sleep and I couldn't. At last, I closed my eyes and did sleep for a few minutes, but before long something began to happen on the inside of me. There was a spiritual battle, and I suffered the most, for my stomach began to turn and toss. Then shortly, I got out of the bed. I was weak because of the spiritual battle that was taking place. I began to crawl from my bed toward the bathroom. I finally stuck my head into the toilet bowl, and sat and vomited for about an hour. I tell you I felt as if my toes were coming out of my throat.

When I finally got to my senses, I said, "Lord, what's wrong?"

When you ask God to show you something, you can be assured that He won't lie to you. He will tell you the truth! He'll show you and guide you to the area of repentance.

The Word came to me as plain as the nose on my face, Ephesians 4:26 says,

Be ye angry, and sin not: let not the sun go down upon your wrath.

Those words kept going over and over and over in my mind.

I said, "But Lord, I didn't sin, it's her fault. You know it's her fault. It wasn't me."

And the Lord said, "Have you looked at yourself in a mirror to see if it could be you?"

I believe it would be worthwhile for us to examine the motives of our hearts before we accuse anyone else of wrong doing. If we think we're so righteous, and if we think we're perfect, then it would help us to see the possibility that we could be wrong and that the other person may be right. This was a shocking revelation to my system.

When I humbled myself, stood up and looked at myself in the mirror, I saw myself in the spirit. It was as though a neon sign was burning across my forehead, saying, "You are wrong, you are wrong, you are wrong, you are wrong!" It didn't take me very long to realize that it was I who had to repent and not my wife. As I repented and asked God's forgiveness I immediately felt better.

By that time my wife heard me groaning in the night and came to help me. After all, being in the toilet bowl for an hour, it was easy to find me! I confessed my faults to her and asked for her forgiveness. She forgave me and led me to our bed.

Well, that's the way the devil is. He'll put your head in a toilet bowl. He'll put you where it stinks. That's where he wants you. But Jesus doesn't want you there. He wants you to prosper and have an abundant life.

In bed she brushed her hand over my forehead and said, "Lord, give him peace," or something to that effect.

I fell asleep right away. When I got up in the morning, I was completely recovered, in my spirit, soul and body.

Narrow-mindedness expresses itself in many different ways and areas. For example, you may become resentful when God starts blessing someone else, or you may be jealous when another brother is being used by God. You may find yourself undermining his ministry, or whatever it is that he may be doing, by talking about him and trying to put him down. You may see a church that God is prospering and you may say, ''Oh, if those people didn't have a gimmick every Sunday, they wouldn't have so many people attending their services.''

People with unrenewed minds are always tring to find fault in someone else, but if God blesses *their* church, well, it's a completely different situation.

That is narrow-mindedness and we need to renew our minds with the Word of God.

7

More Symptoms
of the Unrenewed Mind

Uncontrollable thoughts, vile imaginations, impure pictures, wandering thoughts, confused ideas, and double-mindedness are symptoms of the unrenewed mind. We will discuss each of these symptoms in this chapter.

UNCONTROLLABLE THOUGHTS

How many times have you gone to bed and couldn't sleep? How many times have you had problems with thoughts that you couldn't control. Uncontrollable thoughts are just coming at you and bombarding you, and you have no victory.

I've had that problem, and I'm sharing with you some of the things that have happened to me.

There is no way for you to control these thoughts if you don't want to face them. You say to yourself, "I don't want to think about them any more," and yet you keep thinking the disturbing, or bad thoughts. Who is giving them to you?

If someone else is giving these thoughts to you, and God does not control the minds of His people, then who would it be?

If you are saved and Spirit filled, but you have these thoughts that you cannot control, it is evident that *you* are not in charge of your mind. When these thoughts bombard you and you cannot control them, then *someone else* has the control of your mind.

If you are a Christian you should realize that you are in Christ Jesus. You should take authority and take the thoughts back, and take back your will from whomever has stolen it from you, or to whom you have surrendered your mind, will, and personality.

If you cannot control your bad thoughts, and God is not giving them to you, and you say that you don't want to think these thoughts, then who is giving them to you? Who is putting them in your mind? If they are not coming from God, and they are not coming from you, then they are coming from the *devil himself*.

Someone asks, "Well, how can a Christian be tormented by demons?"

A Christian can and is tormented by demons just like Jesus, Peter, Paul, and others who were tormented by them. These are the *spiritual forces*. That's why the Bible says,

> **For though we walk in the flesh, we do not war after the flesh;**
>
> **(For the *weapons of our warfare* are not carnal, but *mighty through God to the pulling down* of strong holds;)**
>
> **Casting down imaginations and every high thing that exalteth itself against the knowledge of God, and bringing into captivity every *thought* to the obedience of Christ.**
>
> 2 Corinthians 10:3-5

Where are these imaginations?

Where are these strongholds?

They are in your mind.

It's time that you recognize how the enemy will come to attack, and rob you if your mind is not *renewed in God's Word,* and you are not in charge.

VILE IMAGINATIONS, IMPURE PICTURES, WANDERING THOUGHTS

Is your mind controlled or troubled constantly by *vile imaginations, impure pictures,* or *wandering thoughts*?

These are signs or symptoms of the unrenewed mind.

Isaiah said,

Thou wilt keep him in perfect peace, whose mind is stayed on thee: because he trusteth in thee.
Isaiah 26:3

In other words, whoever keeps his mind upon the Lord, him will the Lord keep in perfect peace. You need to keep your mind upon the Lord.

Whenever the devil begins to bombard you with these thoughts, *you can* control them. Here is how I overcame these symptoms.

I knew that those thoughts were not from God, and I had to take charge of them, so I began to think, talk and sing about the Lord. We have a picture in our house, showing Jesus and two of His disciples walking on the Road to Emmaus. As I looked at that picture, I visualized myself standing next to Jesus, looking face to face. Or I saw myself translated into heaven with Jesus. I could see Him sitting on the throne, and I was looking at Him and talking to Him. I tell you when I started thinking like that, *in the spirit,* those impure thoughts left me. I recognized that it was the enemy trying to rob me of my relationship with the Lord.

CONFUSED IDEAS OR DOUBLE-MINDEDNESS

There are born again, Spirit-baptized people who have confused ideas, and they are unable to think clearly, because of double-mindedness.

If you don't have a clear-cut picture when you decide to do something, your mind is confused and then you need to take authority over that situation by confessing that you have the mind of Christ and you are waiting upon the Lord. He will direct you in all things.

When you know *God's will* in your decision, then *stand!*

When you have confused ideas, even though you are a Christian, recognize that they are from the enemy and start reading the Word.

James 1:6 tells us,

But let him ask in faith, nothing wavering. For he that wavereth is like a wave of the sea driven with the wind and tossed.

Verse 8 of the same chapter says,

A double-minded man is unstable in all his ways.

This is speaking about Christians. When a Christian does not know which way to go, he cannot make up his mind, the Bible says he is unstable in all his ways. Verse 7 says,

For let not that man think that he shall receive any thing of the Lord.

When a Christian is unstable in all of his ways, and he can't be trusted, the Bible says that that person is not going to receive anything from God.

You are going to have to rely upon God, and no matter how big the mountain is, your job is to climb the mountain. And it is His job to give you the strength to overcome it. Know this, He has *already overcome* the mountain and *given you power*, and now you are more than a conqueror in Christ Jesus.

If you don't want to think evil or bad thoughts, why do you think them?

I'll tell you why. These are the thoughts of temptation that the enemy has brought into your mind, but only *you* can accept or reject them. *You* are to take control of your mind by *casting down* these thoughts and imaginations and confessing to your mind those things which are true, honest, just, pure, lovely and of good report (Phil. 4:8) — *cause yourself* to think on *these things*. The power of Christ is with you to do this.

8
Controlling Your Mind

Are you in control of your mind?

God does not possess or control the mind of His people. God gave you a mind, and you are a free, moral agent. You have to make up your own mind and decide for yourself what you wish to do, and under whose influence you are, and to whom you are going to submit your mind.

The devil's desire is to get after your mind — to control your mind and your thoughts. Once he has entered into your mind, then he will wait for the proper moment and strike at you when you least expect it.

That's how the devil operates in the mind, which is in the soulish realm.

When you admit that you don't want to think bad thoughts, then it is obvious that someone else controls your mind, and puts those improper thoughts into your mind.

If it is not of God, and you say it is not you, then it has to be of the devil.

If you are a Christian and you are being tormented by the devil, how are you going to overcome him? James 4:7,8 tells us how we can overcome the enemy and live a victorious life with Christ, by submitting ourselves to God and resisting the devil.

> **Submit yourselves therefore to God. Resist the devil, and he will flee from you.**
>
> **Draw nigh to God, and he will draw nigh to you. Cleanse your hands, ye sinners; and purify your hearts, ye double-minded.**

You can be saved and Spirit-filled and still have evil spirits controlling your mind, thoughts and desires.

If you are saved, I know that the devil is after you to destroy you. He will tempt you in every area. Because he tempts you, you need to control your thoughts and guard your mind.

I know there are some who say, "Well, I don't believe that the evil one can control my mind or my fleshly desires."

Jesus says:

> **Love not the world, neither the things that are in the world. If any man love the world, the love of the Father is not in him.**
>
> **For all that is in the world, the lust of the flesh, and the lust of the eyes, and the pride of life, is not of the Father, but is of the world.**
>
> **1 John 2:15,16**

In other words, don't place your eyes upon the things of the world. Because when you place your eyes on the things of the world, you have to take your eyes off Jesus. Jesus said in Matthew 6:33,

> **But seek ye first the kingdom of God, and his righteousness; and all these things shall be added unto you.**

He is telling us to keep our eyes and our minds stayed upon the Lord.

He says, "If any man love the world, then the love of the Father is not in him." He is saying, if any man thinks about the material things *more* than he thinks about God, if he takes his time away that he should give to God, and puts it into the world, a person, a home, or whatever, then the love of God is not in him.

I am not saying that you should not have nice things. I think every Christian ought to have and live the abundant life. You may not have a million dollars, but you ought to live like a millionaire. This is the will of the Father; however, our eyes should not be on the things of the world, but on the Lord, not because you have to, but because He is worthy and you love Him.

This is the difference between a religious person and a Christian person. A religous person is told what to do, and he has to do it, and in many cases he does it whether he wants to or not. A Christian person does it because he loves to do it. God doesn't take your mind and say you have to go to church. God speaks to your heart, and because of your love for Jesus, you do it with joy. But, when an organization dictates to you what you have to do — that is religion. Here is the difference between a will that God controls and a will that someone else controls.

The mind of man is sovereign to man, and God has respect for the mind of man. But there is one who does not respect a man. There is one who doesn't care what happens to you. There is one, the devil, who wants to possess your mind. Satan wants to get into your mind and do a lot of harm, because he knows that once he gets control (of your mind) he will turn you anytime he wants you to turn, just like a rudder on a ship.

Some people will say, "Well, that's impossible. It's unthinkable."

Well, let me tell you, I have seen some saved and Spirit-filled cheaters. I have seen some saved and Spirit-filled liars. I have seen some saved and Spirit-filled Christians who can't get along with anyone. They just had bad dispositions. Some people are difficult to get along with.

I ask you, "Are you difficult to get along with? Is that the *Spirit of the Lord?*" It just couldn't be!

What about the spirit of jealousy, arrogance, backbiting? What about getting on the telephone and gossiping about someone else? Is that Jesus? These are the signs and symptoms that someone else is in control of your mind.

If you have these problems, you should recognize them and go to the Lord and say, "Lord, here are my problems. I bring them to you because you care for me, and I ask you, Jesus, to forgive me and deliver me from them" (Joel 2:32).

Then renew and cleanse your mind with the washing of water by the Word (Eph. 5:26).

9

The Will, the Intellect, and Emotions

Satan is after your will. In order to get to your will, he has to get to your mind. In your mind there is the *will, the emotions*, and the *intellect* which is only one part of you — these three are in the soulish area.

Visualize with me a whole person.

1. This person has a *mind* (or emotions).

2. This person has a *will*.

3. This person has an *intellect*.

Man of course is more than just *soulish* — man is *spirit, soul* and *body*. However, in this chapter I wish to deal with the *soulish* part of man.

Sometimes people say, "How come you are so emotional?"

Well, I'll tell you "how come!" When a person has surrendered his *mind*, his *will*, and his *intellect* to the *Spirit of God* and he gets emotional, he doesn't care what the people think. He only cares what God thinks of him.

Satan is after your mind for one reason. He knows that if he can get to your mind, and get you to think like the world does, and if he can get you to thinking like everybody else does, then you have given him a legal right to enter your mind and dominate your will.

That is why people, even some Christians, many times cannot control the things they do. They know that what they are doing is not pleasing to God. But their answer is, "I just could not help it."

If you can't help it, then you are going to have to recognize that this area has been weakened, and there is someone controlling or influencing your will. But when you call upon the name of the Lord, He will answer you and help you to get your *will* back from the one who stole it from you, or to whom you gave it.

Your *mind,* your *will,* your *intellect,* and your *emotion* are in the soulish realm. Your soul does not have direct fellowship with the Father. That is to say, it is your spirit that has direct fellowship with the Father. Your spirit receives the revelation from the Father by the Holy Spirit. It is the spirit of man within you that is "born again" and not your soul.

Therefore, the object is to cause our soul (the unrenewed mind) to be subject to our spirit. For in our spirit, by the power of the Holy Spirit comes the influence to our soul to do good. And then, of course, the body has no choice but to line up with the Word of God.

There are certain things that we can do with our intellect. But spiritual things come from God the Father. They come into our spirit.

As an individual, you must recognize where the thoughts are coming from. You have to recognize who controls your *will.*

If you are a Christian and have a problem in this area, you must *renew your mind with the Word of God,* and use the spiritual authority and weapons that God has given you and pull down the strongholds that attack your mind.

10
Pulling Down Strongholds

For though we walk in the flesh, we do not war after the flesh:

(For the weapons of our warfare are not carnal, but mighty through God to the pulling down of strongholds;)

Casting down imaginations, and every high thing that exalteth itself against the knowledge of God, and bringing into captivity every thought to the obedience of Christ.

2 Corinthians 10:3-5

If we are going to pull down the strongholds of Satan, we will need to know our position and authority in Christ. Also we need to appropriate proper weapons that God has given us to fight the enemy. You must locate the strongholds of Satan and attack them with the Word of God.

Where are the *strongholds of Satan,* and where do the imaginations occur?

Imaginations occur in our mind when the mind begins to think and imagine things contrary to God's Word. You must then take your *will* and *emotions,* or *intellect* and confess the Word of God to help you expel the negative imaginations which are happening in the mind. You must cast them out.

It is very important that you as a Christian understand these processes. You should know that the enemy is going to attack you in the mind area, and that he will try to get your will and your emotions, to keep you from living a victorious life.

You must put on the full armor of God and be on the *alert* all the time.

Your spirit should always be active and in charge, so that when Satan tries to get into your mind, your spirit will notify your mind and you will resist him with the Word of God.

That is what Jesus did when the devil tempted Him in the wilderness and also through the words of Peter. You see, the Spirit of God that's from within Him, told Him what Satan was trying to do. Jesus didn't read a book about that. He heard the Father's Voice, which came from the depths of His heart to His head. Having recognized the attack of His enemy, He willed to rebuke him with His mouth, saying: "Satan, get thee behind me."

Think for a moment of your mind as a computer that is capable of storing positive or negative information for later recall. You can store the Word of God which has faith and power, or you can store the lies of Satan which are unbelief, fear and doubt.

Whatever you listen to, willingly as an individual, will be stored in your computer (heart).

When you allow an individual who is filled with doubts, negative thoughts and confessions that are contrary to the Word of God to dominate you, and you do nothing to stop them, you are exposing yourself to the great danger of becoming as they are. In Proverbs 23:7 it says, **"For as he thinketh in his heart, so is he...."** Matthew 12:34 reads, **"...for out of the abundance of the heart the mouth speaketh.**

Now suppose you get up in the morning and immediately make a confession contrary to the Word of God. Where did it come from?

I'll tell you where it came from. It came from your heart. Why?

Because you have allowed the *mind* and your *will* to permit negative thoughts to come in and abide in the computer area.

The Bible says:

For by thy words thou shalt be justified, and by thy words thou shalt be condemned.

Matthew 12:37

If I am going to be condemned by my words, and be justified by my words and the thoughts that come into my mind, then I can choose what I want to say. I can say that which will cause my edification, or it can cause me to come to destruction (in my thoughts). I do the choosing with my *will*. *I will to speak. I will not to speak.* Can you see that? *I will to listen,* or *I will not to listen.*

Satan is after one thing, and that is to destroy your spiritual relationship with the Father. However, in order for him to get to your spirit, he will have to go through your mind first. Having gone into your mind, he will now try to take over your will and destroy your spirit.

That is how the enemy tries to come in and dominate persons' lives. Watch your confessions, because

Thou art snared with the words of thy mouth, thou art taken with the words of thy mouth.

Proverbs 6:2

Be very careful, not only of *what* you say, but also of *how* you say it.

Any time that your *soul is in control* instead of your *spirit,* confusion occurs. It is just as though a woman is placed in charge of an entire household. It is not her full responsibility, but many times she is forced into such a situation. When this occurs, nothing seems to go as it should.

The soul is not supposed to be in charge of your whole life. It helps the spirit fight the fleshly desires and to live life victoriously. The *spirit is supposed to be in charge,* just as the husband is supposed to be in charge of the entire household, with the help of the wife, and they work together to produce successful, happy family living.

You must confess whatever you desire, and confess this through the Word of God. Psalm 37:4 reads:

Delight thyself also in the Lord; and He shall give thee the desires of thine heart.

39

> For verily I say unto you, That whosoever shall say unto this mountain, Be thou removed, and be thou cast into the sea; and shall not doubt in his heart, but shall believe that those things which he saith shall come to pass; he shall have whatsoever he saith.
>
> Therefore I say unto you, What things soever ye desire, when ye pray, believe that ye receive them, and ye shall have them.

Mark 11:23,24

That is why Satan wants to destroy positive thoughts in your mind and keep your heart empty. He knows that when the heart is filled with God's Word, it will come out of your mouth!

Again, I ask you, where are the strongholds of Satan? Why is he trying to acquire that position? Some Christians, even Spirit-filled Christians, have allowed Satan to make a *beach-head landing* in their minds, right in the area where he wants. If a saved, Spirit-filled person has evil thoughts controlling and dominating his mind, that person can be taken over at will by the devil whenever he desires.

While in the Armed Forces I was taught that when you hit the enemy beaches you must dig in and establish a foothold.

Once you move in and get a foothold on the beach, you can be sure that you will rout the enemy, and if the enemy is going to rout you, he will have to destroy your foothold and get you off the beach.

Don't you know that Satan works from within just like a fifth column?

Some centuries back (Joshua 6) a servant of God attacked a walled city that no one else was able to defeat. As he and his armies marched to the walled city, I am almost sure that he was asked how he proposed to take the city, and he replied, "I will take it with a *fifth column*," and the reply was: "What do you mean with a *fifth column*? Your troops are to the north, south, east and west. What is this *fifth column business*?" He said, "I am sure, in the city we have our troops. They are in disguise, but they are there nevertheless, and that's how we are going to take the city, when we want to." The devil says, "I am going to take you when I want you, but I am going to take you through a *fifth column.*"

Yes, you are saved and Spirit baptized, but your mind is unrenewed, so the devil can take you whenever he wants to.

There are many persons who are bound in their minds, and the devil has a foothold.

If I were just to tell you that you are not saved, you would probably say, "OK, let's get saved," but tomorrow you would still have your symptoms of narrow-mindedness.

Getting saved is not the answer to the needs of the mind. Of course, it's the *first* step. How can anyone renew their thoughts if they are not born again (saved)?

Let me define a thought: A *thought* is "a mental process when your mind reaches out and grasps at things because it wants to learn and to know."

When your mind is grasping at things, you are doing some thinking and learning. But when something else such as a *fifth column* starts grasping your mind, it is the devil.

People who are being troubled by confused ideas, wandering thoughts, jealousy, envy, gossip and many other different symptoms, are being bothered by the *fifth column*, by the strongholds of Satan.

Satan's power and forces are designed to put evil thoughts into a man's mind and create situations where the evil thoughts will materialize. These forces will try to block off thinking processes to keep you from getting through to God, by putting an evil thought into your own heart. John 13:2 reads:

> **And supper being ended, the *devil having now put into the heart of Judas Iscariot,* Simon's son, to betray him.**

41

There is no doubt in my mind that Judas loved Jesus and had a ministry of casting out devils, healing the sick as did the others. Jesus loved him also and allowed him to be the treasurer, a postition of trust. The Bible reads in Matthew 6:21:

> **For where your treasure is, there will your heart be also.**

Here we can see that they loved and trusted one another and yet the devil having put into the heart of Judas Iscariot to betray Jesus. It is very clear that the devil was given permission to put an evil thought of greed into the heart of a believer.

Now if the devil can put a thought into a believer's heart, he can also take the Word of God out of the believer's heart when he is given an opportunity. Luke 8:12 reads:

> **...then cometh the devil, and taketh away the word out of their hearts, lest they should believe and be saved.**

But the devil cannot inject or put a thought into your mind when you are in control of your mind, and do not have selfish desires and lust after things of this world as Judas did (John 12:4-6).

You can see, I am sure, that Judas was not in control of his mind, and Satan destroyed him. Are you in control of your mind? Where do you stand today my friend? Is there an area in your life that needs to be dealt with?

God does not control the minds of His people. If He did, He would violate His own Word!

The Bible says that God is Love! Love thinketh no evil; love believeth all things; love worketh no evil; love casteth out all fear.

Well how is it that the evil spirits can attack Christians?

Very simply — the Christian allows them to attack himself by giving Satan a foothold in his mind. However, no demon or the devil can have a foothold in our minds when our hearts and minds are renewed according to the Word of God. You are not at the mercy of the devil when you are doing the will of the Father — because greater is He that is within you than he that is in the world.

You are the overcomer, through the Word of Christ Jesus (1 John 5:4,5), but when you give ground to Satan in your mind, then you become a servant of Satan, even though you claim to be saved (Rom. 6:16; John 8:34,35).

I would say that one of the greatest needs for Christians today is to renew their minds. I have never seen, or known a work of God destroyed from without, but I have seen a work of God destroyed from within the body of believers.

You will find that Satan will work on one person with an unrenewed mind, and that person, by the very law of attraction, will attract other unrenewed minds to himself, and very soon a poisonous plot is spreading in the congregation bringing death and destruction to everything it touches.

I have known individuals, and I do know some today, who have lost their healing, even their salvation, because of their unrenewed minds.

How can you have a defense against the devil? Satan knows when your mind is renewed and when it is not, and in order for you not to give ground to the evil forces in your mind, you must renew your mind with the Word of God. Then you can strongly attack with the Word the old areas of Satan and tear down his strongholds. Then, and only then, can you have victory in your life.

Jesus also had problems with the devil. Paul had problems with the devil. Paul said this in Romans 7:19,

For the good that I would I do not; but the evil which I would not, that I do.

The things that he did, he didn't want to do, and the things he should have done, he did not do. He said, "I'm having difficulty, and the thing that causes me to do these things that I don't want to do is the evil in me."

I know, so well, that Paul had problems. I too, have problems, but praise God! I am more than a conqueror through Christ Jesus. I can overcome through Christ, because He has promised a way over our problems.

When bad thoughts are coming into your mind, then the devil has a foothold in your mind. If the devil does have a foothold in your mind, no matter how saved you may be, there is work to be done in your life.

1 Corinthians 10:13 says,

> There hath no temptation taken you but such as is common to man: but God is faithful, who will not suffer you to be tempted above that ye are able; but will with the temptation also make a way to escape, that ye may be able to bear it.

That means He will not allow you to be tempted above what you can stand.

You may ask, "Well, how do I know that Jesus will deliver me from all these temptations, from this fear?"

If you desire Jesus to deliver you from these temptations, fears and these evil thoughts, then go to the Bible. He has given us the promise that He will do this. He is showing us such a beautiful passage that I must rejoice.

I asked the Lord this question, "Lord, how do I know really, that you will deliver me?"

If you come to Jesus and you are sincere with Him, it says that He will deliver you. Here is that Scripture that He gave to us,

> Forasmuch then as the children are partakers of flesh and blood, he also himself likewise took part of the same; that through death he might destroy him that had the power of death, that is the devil.
>
> Hebrews 2:14

Here Jesus is telling us that He willingly came, and He willingly died, that He might take away the sting of death. He broke the sting of death, so that we may have victory through Christ. He said that He has delivered us. He said that He took the power of death from the devil. And in Hebrews 2:15 it reads:

> **And deliver them who through fear of death were
> all their lifetime subject to bondage.**

If you are in bondage with the fear of death, if you have bondage that you are going to die of a particular disease, remember that Jesus died that you may live without fear. He set all of His people free from the bondage of death, because there is no more death for you. You have eternal life.

Why should anyone be afraid of what is going to happen to the flesh?

If the devil is working on you or me in the area of our minds, we can stop him, if we understand that there is no fear in the spiritual realm, but the fear is in the soulish realm. And Satan is after you, trying to put thoughts in your mind that you are going to die from some kind of sickness.

Hebrews 2:16 states:

> **For verily he took not on him the nature of angels;
> but he took on him the seed of Abraham.**

Jesus did not take upon himself the nature of angels, for He came here in the flesh, just as you and I. In Hebrews 2:17 it reads:

> **Wherefore in all things it behoved him to be made
> like unto his brethren. . . .**

Jesus was just like you and me, because we are His brothers. It behooved Him to be made just as we are.

Why?

So that He too could be tempted in all areas. Yes, Jesus has been tempted with everything the devil had. But Jesus said to him, **It is written** (Luke 4:4). Jesus knew the Word. He came at the devil with the Word, *because there is power in that Word*. Jesus came at the devil with the Word, but He walked in the flesh just as you and I. When he was nailed to the cross, it hurt Him in the flesh, in His hands and in His feet, and in His side.

45

But He said, **Father, forgive them; for they know not what they do** (Luke 23:34).

Can you and I display such love as did Jesus?

He was just as human as you are today, and yet He was just as much God as He was human. He knows how you and I feel. He knows the temptations. Jesus suffered that you might be set free.

Jesus overcame all of that in the mind, because He surrendered His will to the Father. He wasn't thinking as the world thinks. He was thinking as His Heavenly Father thinks — for He says, **With men this is impossible; but with God all things are possible** (Matt. 19:26).

Then He said in Hebrews 2:17,

> ...**that he might be a merciful and faithful high priest in things pertaining to God, to make reconciliation for the sins of the people.**

Jesus is your high priest. Jesus is the one who understands you better than anybody else. He understands you better than you understand yourself. That is why He is like He is and is where He is.

Hebrews 2:18 tells us,

> **For in that he himself hath suffered being tempted, he is able to succour them that are tempted.**

That is why I know that Jesus will provide a way for you and me to escape, because He too was tempted. He is able to secure them that are tempted and make them free.

John 8:31-32 reads:

> ...**If ye continue in my word, then are ye my disciples indeed.**
>
> **And ye shall know the truth, and the truth shall make you free.**

I am completely convinced that it is not the magnitude of man's intelligence that gives him problems when God begins to deal with his heart and the symptoms of the unrenewed mind, but the lack of development in that area.

God has promised to transform our hearts and illuminate our intellect when we become His disciples. He will continue to renew our minds as we continue in His Word, and the joy of the Lord will be our daily strength.

To contact the author,
write:
Bill Basansky
Love and Grace Fellowship
P. O. Box 7126
Fort Myers, Florida 33911

Please include your prayer requests and comments when you write.

Additional copies are available
at your local bookstore
or by writing:

Harrison House
P. O. Box 35035 • Tulsa, OK 74153

For additional copies
of this book
in Canada contact:

Word Alive
P. O. Box 670
Niverville, Manitoba
CANADA R0A 1EO